Hong Kong is fast-p...............................e
talent combines wit...........
portunity, be it in de............
food, and judging th............
undermine its large ....
approachable, Hong Kong seamlessly connects Asia to the rest of
the world.

CITIx60: Hong Kong explores the Asian powerhouse in five aspects,
covering architecture, art spaces, shops and markets, eating and
entertainment. With expert advice from 60 stars of the city's creative scene, this book guides you to the real attractions of the city
for an authentic taste of Hong Kong life.

Contents

Before You Go

BASIC INFO

Currency
HK Dollar (USD/$)
Exchange rate: US$1 : HK$7.8

Time zone
GMT +8

Hong Kong does not observe DST.

Dialling
International calling: +852

Weather (avg. temperature range)
Spring (Mar-Apr): 16-23°C / 61-73°F
Summer (May-Aug): 23-33°C / 73-91°F
Autumn (Sep-Nov): 19-30°C / 66-86°F
Winter (Dec-Feb): 10-20°C / 50-68°F

*Typhoon season runs roughly from June to
September. Most public transport suspends
service when signal T8 or higher is in force.

USEFUL WEBSITES / NUMBER

Hong Kong-Macau ferry services
crossboundaryferryservices.mardep.gov.hk

Weather forecasts & typhoon warnings
www.hko.gov.hk

Public transport routes & fares
www.td.gov.hk

24-hour free hotline for lost property on taxi
187 2920

EMERGENCY CALLS

Ambulance, fire or police
999

Consulates
Japan   +852 2522 1184
France   +852 3752 9900
Germany   +852 2105 8788
UK   +852 2901 3000
US   +852 2523 9011

AIRPORT EXPRESS TRANSFER

**Hong Kong International Airport <-> Central
(Airport Express)**
Trains / Journey: every 10-12 mins / 24 mins
From airport – 0554-0048
From HK station – 0550-0059
One-way: $100, round trip (valid for 30 days): $180
www.mtr.com.hk

Hong Kong International Airport <-> Central (A11)
Bus / Journey: every 15-30 mins / 50 mins
From airport – 0610-0030
From North Point Ferry Pier – 0510-2230
One-way: $40
www.nwstbus.com.hk

PUBLIC TRANSPORT IN HONG KONG

Metro
Bus
Light bus
Taxi
Tram
Ferry

Means of Payment
Octopus card
Cash

*Free or discounted bus-bus interchange ap-
plies to Octopus card users at selective routes.
Red topped light buses may accept cash only.

GENERAL PUBLIC HOLIDAYS

January	1 New Year's Day
February	Chinese New Year*
April	4/5 Ching Ming Festival, Good Friday, Easter Monday
May	1 Labour Day, Buddha's birthday*
June	Tuen Ng Festival
July	1 HKSAR Establishment Day
September	Day after Mid-Autumn Festival*
October	1 National Day, Chung Yeung Festival*
December	25 Christmas Day, 26 Boxing Day

*Holidays observe Chinese calendars and vary by
year. Galleries and shops normally close for 1-15
days from the first day of Chinese New Year.

FESTIVALS / EVENTS

January
Hong Kong Marathon
www.hkmarathon.com
Fotanian Open Studios
FB: FotanianOpenStudios

March
Hong Kong International Film Festival
www.hkiff.org.hk
ifva Festival
www.ifva.com
Art Basel HK
www.artbasel.com

May
Chai Wan Mei: Art & Design Festival
www.chaiwanmei.com

July
ACGHK
www.ani-com.hk

October
New Vision Arts Festival
www.newvisionfestival.gov.hk
Social Innovation Festival
www.10dayfest.hk

November
Clockenflap
www.clockenflap.com
Microwave Festival
www.microwavefest.net
Oxfam Trailwalker
www.oxfamtrailwalker.org.hk
Kowloon City Book Fair
kowlooncitybookfair.creativehk.edu.hk

December
deTour
www.detour.hk
JCCAC Festival (#16)
www.jccac.org.hk
TOY SOUL
www.toysoul.hk

Event days vary by year. Please check for
updates online.

UNUSUAL OUTINGS

Harbour Runners
harbourrunners.hk

Walk In Hong Kong
www.walkin.hk

Lawnmap
lawnmaphk.org

Secret Tour HK
www.facebook.com/secrettourhk

Geopark tour
www.geopark.gov.hk

Photography tour
photoblog.hk

SMARTPHONE APP

Comprehensive restaurant directory & reviews
Openrice

Commute planners
MTR Mobile, KMB & LW, Citybus NWFB

Taxi request & pick-up
Easy Taxi

Hike route profiles & environmental monitoring
TrailWatch

REGULAR EXPENSES

Newspaper
$7

Domestic / International mail (postcards)
$1.7/$2.3

Gratuities
Diners: 10% service charge inclusive
Hotels: $10-20 for porter & cleaners at one's
discretion

Count to 10

What makes Hong Kong so special?

Illustrations by Guillaume Kashima aka Funny Fun

Hong Kong may be known for its bright lights and tall buildings, but when done well, it's remembered for its addictive food and heavenly hikes. Here, world culture and traditions mingle and deliver unique character. Whether you are on a one-day stopover or a week-long stay, see what Hong Kong creatives consider essential to see, taste, read and take home from your trip.

1

Architecture

HSBC Headquarters
by Norman Foster

Bank of China Tower
by I. M. Pei & Partners

Central Elevated Walkway System
by HKSAR

Government Headquarters
by Rocco Design Architects

Jardine House
by Palmer and Turner Hong Kong

Walled villages
Tsang Dai Uk, Ping Shan, Kat Hing Wai

Public housing estates
*Yue Kwong Chuen, Choi Hung Estate,
Wah Fu Estate*

2

Old Chinese Tradition

Tai Ping Ching Chiu
www.wikipedia.org/wiki/Dajiao

Bun mountain snatching
Cheung Chau Bun Festival

Ghost festival
*Burn paper offerings,
Chinese opera, food fair, etc.*

Cantonese opera
Sunbeam Theatre

Fire Dragon Dance
Tai Hang or Pokfulam

**Make Chinese New Year
Wishes**
*Che Kung Temple,
Wong Tai Sin Temple*

Villain hitting
*Canal Rd, Causeway Bay
(underneath Canal Rd. Flyover)*

3

Neighbourhood Staples

Egg waffle
Lee Keung North Point Egget
GF, 178 Nathan Rd., Tsim Sha Tsui

Buttered pineapple bun
Kowloon Restaurant
282 Yu Chau St., Sham Shui Po

Sugar cane juice & jelly
Kung Lee
60 Hollywood Rd., Central

Clay Pot Rice
Kun Kee
*243-5 Des Voeux Rd. W.,
Western District*

Barbecued roasts
Joy Hing Roasted Meats
265-7 Hennessy Rd., Wan Chai

Hotpot
Hung Fook Seafood & Hotpot
86 Lok Shan Rd., To Kwa Wan

4

Tea Culture

Zen tearoom
House of Moments
FB: moments.teahouse

Modern tearoom
Teakha
Teakha.com

Neighbourhood cafés
Australian Dairy Company
47 Parkes St., Jordan

Dragon Ball Jasmine Tea
Ying Kee Tea House
www.yingkeetea.com

Tea tasting & workshops
Ming Cha Tea House
www.mingcha.com

Tea ware showcase & meal
Flagstaff House Museum Of
Tea Ware & Lock Cha

5

Local Crafts & Manufacturing

Folk crafts & ceramics
PMQ (#25): See Through Craftsmen

Paper offerings
Queen's Rd. W., Sheung Wan
Canton Rd., Yau Ma Tei

Bamboo scaffolding
Everywhere

Qipao tailoring
Mee Wah Qipao
meewahqipao.wordpress.com

Letterpress printing
Zi Wut
FB: Zi Wut

Wedding gowns & embroidery
Koon Nam Wah
www.koonnamwah.com.hk

Kung Fu shoes
Tang Shoes Specialty Store
Hollywood Rd., Sheung Wan

6

Design Books & Zines

Lok Man Rare Books
www.lokmanbooks.com

Basheer Design Books
FB: Basheer Design Books HK

Flow books
FB: Flow Bookshop

Kubrick BC (#22)
www.kubrick.com.hk

Page one
FB: Page One HK

ACO Books (#15)
www.aco.hk

Keng Seng Trading & Co. Ltd.
www.kengseng.com

Open Quote @PMQ (#25)
FB: Open Quote

7

Film Locations in HK Movies

Central-Mid-levels Escalator & Walkway System
ChungKing Express (1994)
by Wong Kar-wai

YMCA Bridges St Centre, Soho
Running on Karma (2003)
by Johnnie To, Wai Ka-fai

The Verandah, Repulse Bay
Lust, Caution (2007)
by Ang Lee

St. Joseph's Chapel, Sai Kung
The Killer (1989)
by John Woo

Mei Foo Sun Chuen, Mei Foo
A Simple Life (2011),
July Rhapsody (2001)
by Ann Hui

Jumbo Kingdom, Aberdeen
God of Cookery (1996)
by Lee Lik-chi, Stephen Chow

8
Dimensional City Views

Skyline
on Star Ferry (#59), or from underneath Island Eastern Corridor

Harbour view
Lugard Rd., Victoria Peak

Tour along original coastline
(Sheung Wan <-> Quarry Bay) by tram

Bus ride between 10/F apartments on Hill Rd Flyover
by bus 37X, 90B or 970x from Pok Fu Lam Rd. (East bound)

Lantau & the Big Buddha
from Ngong Ping 360 cable car

Deep Water Bay & Mansions
from Ocean Park cable car

A calm financial district at night
from Chater Garden or Star Ferry Multistorey Carpark (next to City Hall)

9
Getting Close to Nature

Dragon's Back Ridge
Shek O

Yuen Tsuen Ancient Trail
Tsuen Wan

MacLeHose Trail & Big Wave Bay
Sai Kung

Sunset Peak
Lantau Island (esp in autumn)

Po Toi
Southernmost of Hong Kong

Hong Kong Wetland Park
Tin Shui Wai
www.wetlandpark.gov.hk

Geoparks
www.geopark.gov.hk

10
Mementos

HK$20 plimsolls
Grocery stores / markets

Wool Undershirt
Lee Kung Man Retailer
111 Wing Lok St., Sheung Wan

Rattan cane
Old fashioned grocery stores

Chinese Calligraphy Supplies & Inscription
Hong Kong Wah Gor Calligraphy Society (by appointment only)
wahgor.hk

HK Honey & So–Soap products
Kubrick BC/ Kapok
3 Sun St., Wan Chai

Shrimp paste
Tai O

Red–white–blue nylon canvas
Sham Shui Po

Icon Index

 Opening hours   Admission

 Address   Facebook

 Contact   Website

 Remarks

 Scan QR codes to access Google Maps and discover the area around each destination. Internet connection required.

60x60

60 Local Creatives x 60 Hotspots

From vast cityscapes to the tiniest glimpses of everyday exchange, there is much to provoke creative juices. 60x60 points you to 60 haunts where 60 arbiters of taste develop their nose for the good stuff.

Landmarks & Architecture   SPOTS · 01 – 12

Allow yourself to get swept away by the iconic skyline of Hong Kong. Whether you decide to enjoy the scenery by ferry, tram, or on a hike, you won't be disappointed.

Cultural & Art Spaces   SPOTS · 13 – 24

Join art hungry Hongkongers on a gallery tour. Spaces might be intimate, but much is packed in and that is to be admired.

Markets & Shops   SPOTS · 25 – 36

Hong Kong redefines what it is to shop, but there's plenty more than flashy designer flagships. Try a local food market or sniff out vintage finds.

Restaurants & Cafés   SPOTS · 37 – 48

A true foodie haven, Hong Kong delivers on both the familiar and comforting and then in the next bite takes you extremes from your comfort zone.

Nightlife   SPOTS · 49 – 60

In this restless city, the choice of what you can do is as diverse as you want it to be. Plan plenty whether your focus is a night of food, drinking, clubbing or even sport.

Landmarks & Architecture

Shining aspirational buildings, bamboo architecture and war relics

Diverse in characters and forms, the medley of glass-clad towers that girdle Victoria Harbour spells the city's sprightly nature, and tightly-packed settlements its population expansion after WWII. Height in the modern designs effectively captures attention in this crammed city, and speed of new constructions gives the impression of a place always morphing. While star architects like Foster & Partners, Paul Rudolph, Harry Seidler, I.M Pei & Partners and Daniel Libeskind, flock here to fly the flag for their design visions, local architects also exert their creative power building public facilities and re-energising historical architecture across the territory.

Besides visiting omnipresent colonial structures like the former Legislative Council Building (*8 Jackson Rd., Central*), going sightseeing reveals intriguing housing designs, such as stilt houses (Tai O), walled villages (Northern districts), stepped tenement buildings (Jordan, Quarry Bay, Causeway Bay), modular public housing (Tin Shui Wai, Aberdeen), rooftop slums (Sham Shui Po) and listed mansions like King Yin Lei (*45 Stubbs Rd, Happy Valley*) built during the 1930s.

For thrill-seekers, a unique way to take in the views is by climbing a skyscraper as a typhoon hits – an experience that is literally bone-shaking. If you fancy a hike, view Kowloon's low-rises from Lion Rock. Buildings here were stunted under height restrictions when Hong Kong's Kai Tak Airport was in operation between 1925–1998, and offer a distinctly different vista.

Lio Yeung
Founder, Young & Innocent

Seeing commercials as another form of art, Young & Innocent presents print and digital campaigns. Yeung's first exhibition "A is Green, R is Red," was held at the Agnès b LIBRAIRIE GALERIE.

Jockey Club Innovation Tower P.014

Run Run Shaw Creative Media Centre P.015

Joel Chu
Founder, Communion W

Chu is a creative director who founded the design firm Communion W. He's also a dog lover, advocate of simple good design, and is fond of eating, sleeping and shopping.

Bryant Lu
Architect, Ronald Lu & Partners

I am the leader of Ronald Lu & Partners and a father. Life and design come from appreciating the little enjoyment in our daily life. I love good food and heli-skiing, ideally in the same day.

Pak Tsz Lane Park P.016

Joey Ho
Founder, Joey Ho Design Limited

Born in Taiwan, raised in Singapore, Ho gained his Master's in architecture from the University of Hong Kong. Since 2002, his firm has been recognised worldwide.

Chi Lin Nunnery P.017

Bamboo Theatre P.020

Singchin Lo
Founder, PLOTZ

Founding PLOTZ in 2007, Lo believes folds, dips, waves, and knots are integral to tailoring. Lo is a 2014 Asahi Kasei Chinese Fashion Designer Creativity Award winner, and a Woolmark Prize nominee 2013.

Johan M Persson
Founder, C'monde Studios

Persson founded C'monde Studios. The award-winning Swedish industrial design company provides sophisticated elegant designs across a range of markets.

Tai Long Wan P.021

Eric Schuldenfrei & Marisa Yiu
Founding partners, ESKYIU

ESKYIU is a multidisciplinary architectural firm with focuses on designs that articulately integrate our culture with technology.

Yau Ma Tei Wholesale Fruit Market
P.023

Kenji Wong
Founder, GrowthRing & Co.

Formerly Wudai Shiguo's creative director, Wong now helms creative agency, GrowthRing & Co. and furniture shop, GrowthRing & Supply.

Henry Chu
Founder, Pill & Pillow

Henry Chu is a web designer and new media artist, who founded design studio pill & pillow.

Graham Street Market
P.022

Yau Ma Tei Carpark Building
P.024

Romain Jacquet-Lagrèze
Photographer

Amazed by HK's unique urban development, French-born Jacquet-Lagrèze has worked on several series focusing on the city, including *Vertical Horizon* (2012) and *Wild Concrete* (2014).

Mt Davis WWII Batteries & Bunkers
P.026

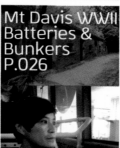

Yang Yeung
Founder, Soundpocket

I teach classics at the Chinese University of Hong Kong, and write about contemporary art and culture in Hong Kong. Sometimes, I curate; sometimes I wander. Hong Kong is my home.

Michael Young
Founder, Michael Young Studio

Michael Young is an industrial designer working in the areas of product, furniture and interior design with studios in Hong Kong and Brussels.

Wild Concrete
P.025

Jewish Cemetery
P.027

1 Jockey Club Innovation Tower

Map I, P.107

Just completed in 2014, the Jockey Club Innovation Tower is a definite eye-catcher at
Hong Kong Polytechnic University's claret-red
campus. Designed by Zaha Hadid Architects,
the visionary building is conceived as a molten
blend of design culture and university life.
Not only do interior and exterior courtyards
provide an airy, light-filled learning space, but
also exhibition areas and communal zones
designed to look inviting for students and staff
to socialise.

🕘 0900–2130 (M–Sa) 🏠 Hong Kong Polytechnic
University, 11 Yuk Choi Rd., Hung Hom
🔗 www.sd.polyu.edu.hk

"Go in July for the design school's graduation show,
and in October for 10-day Fest, when international
artist and designers convene."

– Lio Yeung, Young & Innocent

2 Run Run Shaw Creative Media Centre

Map J, P.107

Like a twinned quartz crystal cluster, the Daniel Libeskind building houses three academic departments and the School of Creative Media (SCM) of the City University of Hong Kong. The design is a crisscross of the horizontal and vertical. Horizontally it is a landscape of space. Vertically it is a landscape of light. The form of the building ascends obliquely capturing Hong Kong's creative spirit and intensity. SCM regularly runs public programmes to explore multimedia and sound art. Revel in the open views to Kowloon from its rooftop.

🕐 *0830–2300 (M–Sa) except semester breaks, summer terms, and public holidays (wk 1–12)*
🏠 *18 Tat Hong Ave., Kowloon Tong*
URL *www.scm.cityu.edu.hk*

"Libeskind's design is like a breath of fresh air in this jungle of uniform and hideous architecture. It's a paragon of imagination and creativity."

– Joel Chu, Communion W

3. Pak Tsz Lane Park

Map C, P.103

In a quiet square of Soho, stands Pak Tsz Lane Park a 19th century site of revolution where anti-Qing societies led by Yeung Ku-wan (1861-1901) and Sun Yat-sen (1866-1925) had secret meetings. Ronald Lu & Partners were tasked in 2009 with redesigning the space to honour the historical significance of the site, using the design theme "Origin of Chinese Revolution". The modern landscaped enclosure has three areas: a pavilion, exhibition space and themed play area where visitors can walk through history through the terraced terrain. The wooden walkways were designed by Gravity Green.

🏠 *Pak Tsz Ln., Soho (Enter from Aberdeen St. & Gage St.)*

"It is part of the Dr. Sun Yat Sen Historical Trail. As you walk along the lane, you'll see many landmarks that hold great significance in Chinese history."

– Bryant Lu, Ronald Lu & Partners

📍4 Chi Lin Nunnery
Map K, P.107

Bounded by an expansive Chinese garden and backed by a ferny hill, this stately buddhist complex is a genuine model of Tang dynasty architecture and the result of a major refurbishment in 1990. Over the span of 33,000 square metres, temple halls entirely built on timber with intricate bracketed roofs are symmetrically laid out in tiers, with elegant stone pathways linking courtyards and gates. Amble through the nunnery to contemplate the numerous statues and "pure land". South to the nunnery lies Nan Lian Garden. At a quiet corner of the park behind a waterfall, Chi Lin Vegetarian serves reputed meat-free fare.

🕐 0900-1630 daily, Chi Lin Vegetarian: 1200-1500, 1800-2100 (M-F), 1130-2100 (Sa-Su & P.H.)
🏠 5 Chi Lin Dr., Diamond Hill 📞 +852 2354 1888
🔗 www.chilin.org (Chi only)

Chi Lin Vegetarian in Nan Lian Garden (top)
Pavilion of Absolute Perfection in Nan Lian Garden (bottom)

"It's free for visitors, and they can also try the vegetarian restaurant nearby."

– Joey Ho, Joey Ho Design Limited

5 Bamboo Theatre

Entirely constructed from bamboo poles and nylon canvas, these sturdy makeshift stages (locally referred to as "bamboo sheds") used for Cantonese opera are a bright cultural spectacle. West Kowloon Bamboo Theatre is perhaps the most splendid example considering its large seating capacity, harbour front location and modernised design but the Xiqu Centre is expected to replace this flagship programme when it completes construction in 2016. Smaller bamboo theatres can still be found in locales like Tai O and Sai Kung, and are erected around various gods' birthdays.

⊕ $ Showtime, date, admission & location vary with year URL www.lcsd.gov.hk/CE/CulturalService/ab/en/bamboo_theatre.php

"Taking the effort of 10 scaffolders and 10,000s of sticks constructed in just 2 weeks, West Kowloon's edition has been the most seminal of its kind in the city for the last 30 years."

– Singchin Lo, PLOTZ

6 Tai Long Wan
Map S, P.110

Nature and white sandy beaches are probably not often what first time visitors associate with Hong Kong. However, far up in a north eastern corner of Sai Kung this is just what you will find. A popular destination for summer junk trips and surfing in the winter months, Tai Long Wan can be reached by a 90-minute hike up the MacLehose Trail section 2, starting from Sai Wan Pavilion. Alternatively, book a water taxi at Sai Kung Pier for a breezy round trip. Ask for assistance at one of Ham Tin Wan's snack places and grab a spontaneous ride.

URL www.discoverhongkong.com, www.oasistrek.com ⚲ Trail begins at Sai Wan Village, near Sai Wan Pavilion, accessible by taxi or village bus service (NR29/29R: 16 Chan Man St.): www.td.gov.hk

"It's one of the few places in the territory where you can find yourself alone. Dig out your old camping gear and spend the night star gazing."

– Johan Persson, C'monde Studios

7 Graham Street Market
Map C, P.103

With over 170 years of history, fishmongers, vegetable stalls, shoemakers and grocers continue to liven Graham Street, at the oldest open-air wet market located at the heart of the frenetic Central Soho district. Although many have been evicted due to redevelopment plans, the 40 some surviving vendors that sprawl across Gage Street win over white collar workers, domestic helpers and chefs everyday with the freshest produce, homemade sauces and dry goods. Get down there fast and early to experience a part of the city's neighbourhood life. The streets are literally wet. Go prepared.

🕑 0700–1600 daily 📍 Graham St., Central

"This is an authentic and lively testament to the real Hong Kong. Our other favourite markets include the Goldfish Market in Mongkok, which sells tropical fish."
– Eric Schuldenfrei & Marisa Yiu, ESKYIU

8 Yau Ma Tei Wholesale Fruit Market

Map I, P.106

An authentic slice of Hong Kong life at this gallery of local fruit traders. With most architectural details still intact, stories of its corrupt past involving triads and drugs in the 1970s can be traced throughout this 1.5-hectare Grade II listed pre-WWII establishment. Take in the ornate rooftops and stained booth signs, to their iron gates, *fengshui* arrangement, and background sounds that mix loud chats with mahjong games. Come here now before it's relocated. Arrive after midnight for a totally different view when Waterloo Road is jam-packed with fruit boxes and busy beefy workmen.

🏠 *Shek Lung St., Yau Ma Tei*
🔗 *Unofficial guided tour: www.walkin.hk*

"Between 4–6am every day, the market becomes a hive of activity that best depicts how locals make their livelihoods. Remember to stay out of the way while you're there."

– Kenji Wong, GrowthRing & Co.

9 Yau Ma Tei Carpark Building
Map I, P.106

An ever-expanding population spills from pavements and has resulted in bizarre architecture like the Yau Ma Tei Carpark Building. Born from a tactical move to make practical use of the space, the project, completed in 1977, was an unprecedented attempt that commanded new techniques to integrate an unforeseen structure into an operational building. The only bus that takes the overpass is N368. Adjacent to the building is Grade I listed Tin Hau Temple complex and *Yung Shue Tau* (Banyan's head), a public square where the residents while away the day with naps, chess or open-air concerts.

🕐 *24 hours* 🏠 *250 Shanghai St., Yau Ma Tei*

"Since it's a carpark, I used to wonder if cars could directly access the flyover from the building when I was a kid."

– Henry Chu, pill & pillow

10 Wild Concrete

Wild Concrete is not a single destination but rather an incredible phenomenon witnessed in many areas of Hong Kong's urban jungle, where trees demonstrate resilience in growing through, in and around buildings. Jacquet-Lagrèze has documented multiple sites around Hong Kong capturing everything from the roots of trees engulfing a housing block to shrubbery sprouting from a rooftop. This beautiful wonder shows the collision of nature and humans through the built environment and a secret struggle for space.

📍 *Reclamation St., Temple St., Yau Ma Tei*
🔗 *All pictures by Romain Jacquet-Lagrèze*

"These trees are unfortunately disappearing quite quickly because the buildings on which they are growing are either collected, demolished or renovated."

– Romain Jacquet-Lagrèze

11 Mt Davis WWII Batteries & Bunkers

Map A, P.102

Located on the westernmost hill of Hong Kong Island are the remains of an old British battery built at the turn of the century to fortify the island from attacks. Although damaged badly from Japanese bombs during the Second World War, the bunker and arsenal endure a formidable presence, and are with their weathered concrete structures, rusted bars, graffiti-clad walls and tangle of wild plants. Take a hike along the Mount Davis Heritage Trail and you will see not just one, but many former military bunkers alongside fantastic views of Victoria Harbour.

🏠 *Mt Davis Path, Pok Fu Lam*

"A quiet and meandering walk; good for listening and reflecting on our past and our present."

– Yang Yeung, Soundpocket

12 Jewish Cemetery
Map B, P.102

Established in 1855 on farmland, this cemetery aimed to serve Hong Kong's Jewish community. The land was leased by the British Crown to a Jewish family that initiated the space in Happy Valley. Concealed from the street, inside the cemetery are 300 well preserved, mostly Sephardic graves, raised from the ground, with some dating back to the late 19th century. Sixteen of the oldest graves bear no name. Admire the Hebrew inscriptions in marble plaques, granite sarcophagi's and aged tombs – the remains of some of Hong Kong's earliest European settlers.

🕐 0800–1800 daily
🏠 13 Shan Kwong Rd., Happy Valley

"My thoughtful place."
– Michael Young, Michael Young Studio

Cultural & Art Spaces

Short-term initiatives, art colonies and world's first Asian art archive

With famously high rents and a government only now tuning into art and creativity (formally it appeared more intent on erasing street art) it's unlikely to find the bustling art scenes of London or New York are to be replicated here any time soon. Instead, art hungry individuals can be found testing ideas at warehouse spaces, rooftops and locales like Fotan, Sham Shui Po (#19), Wong Chuk Hang (#14), and Chai Wan. Artistic visionaries (#15, #17) should be credited for supporting new local artists and preserving public culture by initiating discussions and research. Defunct buildings such as the old Central Police Station (*10 Hollywood Rd., Central*) and disused public spaces like Kwun Tong Ferry Pier are being progressively taken over by small art festivals and programmes, creating a one-of-its-kind cultural experience in Hong Kong.

Besides contemporary art, traditional art like Cantonese opera can be admired at Sunbeam Theatre (*423 King's Rd., North Point*) or bamboo theatres (#5). Explore Soho and Art Basel for more commercial arts and Sheung Wan for mixed inspirations. ARTMAP (*www.artmap.com.hk*) and Timetable (*timable.com*) are two platforms to access regular updates about exhibitions, workshops, artist talks, publications and screenings in town.

Hung Lam
Co-founder, CoDesign & CoLAB

At times I'm a designer, and on occasions I'm a creator. When I'm not making art, you might find me distributing herbal tea.

I'mperfect Xchange @O!! P.032

Spring Workshop P.034

Jeff Leung
Independent curator

Leung organises exhibitions and writes reviews for overseas art magazines. Curatorial work includes "Arte Hiking" (2010) and "1+1: Four Regions Two Strait Artistic Exchange Project" (2011).

Ho Sin Tung
Illustrator

I'm a Fine Art graduate of the Chinese University of Hong Kong. My works are sometimes exhibited, sometimes collected, and sometimes abandoned.

Art & Cultural Outreach P.036

Leumas To
Illustrator, designer & curator

I'm the creator of the Romantic Good Children illustration series (2011), joint exhibitions "5 Patterns" and "10 Patterns" (2012), and collective comics magazine Ping Pong (2014–).

JCCAC P.037

Asia Art Archive P.038

Studio TM
Creative studio

Founded in 2010, Studio TM is the brainchild of Topaz Leung and Martin Cheung. Their major disciplines include photography, advertising, art direction and art education.

Craig Au Yeung
Illustrator, writer & curator

Whether in words, images, comics, or speeches, Au Yeung's works convey flavours, memories and dreams. Markets, dining tables, kitchenware and people's devotion to food are all precious to him.

Sin Sin P.039

Wong Ping
Animator

Besides personal animation works, Wong also writes and directs music videos. His works have been screened internationally and were featured at The Saatchi & Saatchi New Directors' Showcase 2013.

Above Second
P.042

Used Pencil
Illustrator

I emphasise beauty, highlight predicaments and poke fun at humans and their strange habits. Drawing on our social scene and contemporary culture, I create images that reflect the modern world.

Gary Tong
Founder, TGIF

Born in HK and schooled in LA, Tong began his creative career at the Alan Chan Design Company and founded TGIF in 2010. Received awards include a Red Dot Award and Graphic Design in China Awards.

Wontonmeen
P.040

Fringe Club
P.043

John Ho
Illustrator & graphic designer

Devoted to painting, Ho has works published and exhibited in Hong Kong, Japan and the Mainland China.

Jao Tsung-I Academy
P.046

My Little Airport
Band

Songwriter Ah P and vocalist nicole Oujian form indie pop band, My Little Airport. Since 2004, the duo has published nearly 100 original works, mostly focusing on Hong Kong.

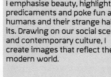

Kila Cheung
Illustrator

Cheung illustrates and sculpts. It's his belief that curiosity and the nerve to resist the conventional, essentially will do good to one's growth. One should also find time to dream.

Broadway Cinematheque & Kubrick BC
P.044

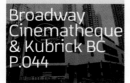

Mapopo Community Farm
P.047

13 I'mperfect Xchange @Oil
Map F, P.105

Since 2012, I'mperfect has been one of CoDesign's collaborative initiatives and promotes
sustainable living and social harmony. Lodged
into the Oil Street Art Space, this community
space opens five days a week to engage and
inspire the public to look twice, through talks,
workshops, laughter clubs and more. A free
glass of herbal tea and a paper coaster adds a
little personal dialogue. While you're there, take
time to explore the red-brick building, now
a community art space converted from the
former Royal Hong Kong Yacht Club clubhouse
built in 1908.

🕐 1200–2000 (W–Su)　🏠 Oil, 12 Oil St., Fortress Hill
📞 +852 2510 8710　f I'mperfect

"Most suitable for you abounding in imperfections."

– Hung Lam, CoDesign

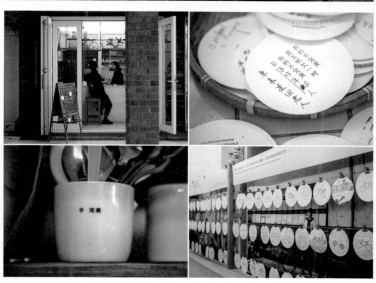

14 Spring Workshop
Map N, P.109

Founded by Mimi Brown, with Defne Ayas as the curator-at-large, Spring aims to unite multidisciplinary art forms in one of the city's few surviving industrial areas. Temporary and nonprofit, the massive space hosts artists in residence, exhibitions, performances and talks with local art groups and international artists. Interact with Industrial Forest by ESKYIU, an experimental garden that acknowledges the area's origin and transformation with hundreds of thin malleable metallic bamboo poles. Also visit the 'Bibliotheek' a curated collection of books, marking the beginning of a permanent library.

🕐 1200–1800 (Tu–Su except between exhibitions)
🏠 3F Remex Ctr., 42 Wong Chuk Hang Rd., Aberdeen
☎ +852 2110 4370 [URL] www.springworkshop.org

"An artistic 'loft living' temperament emanates from the walls of this privately funded space. Beware – they only open their doors when something's on."
– Jeff Leung

15 Art & Cultural Outreach
Map D, P.104

Amid Wan Chai's chaotic streets and blaring car horns is a space where no voice is too loud or offbeat. Since 2003, ACO has remained steadfast in promoting sustainability, social awareness and reading. Movie screenings, mini concerts, exhibitions and book launches take place year-round at the bookshop next to a garden that sustains ACO's food project. Supported by Dawei Charitable Foundation, the multistorey Foo Tak Building has grown into a vertical artist colony, providing an operation base to some 20 writers, painters, crafters and initiatives.

🕐 1200–2000 (Tu–Sa) 🏠 14F, Foo Tak Bldg., 365–367 Hennessy Rd., Wan Chai 📞 +852 2893 4808
URL www.aco.hk 🔗 Cash only

"It's a shelter for experimental arts, where things of all kinds coexist; sales become a remedy for consumption; independent artists are interdependent."

– Ho Sin Tung

16 JCCAC
Map L, P.108

Operating as a self-financed, registered char-
ity, the Jockey Club Creative Arts Centre (JCCAC)
houses studios and convertible spaces where
art practitioners create and interact with the
public. The building itself is a repurposed 1970s
flat-roofed factory building, a telling mix of the
functionality and the glories of the city's by-
gone cottage industries. A regular programme
of exhibitions, performances, rooftop cinemas,
workshops and weekend fairs is open for public viewing. Individual studios accept visitors by
appointment only. Its quarterly handicrafts fair
is a rare platform for individuals to bring their
work into public view.

🕐 1000–2200 daily
🏠 30 Pak Tin St., Shek Kip Mei
📞 +852 2353 1311
URL www.jccac.org.hk

*"Head to the rooftop for an open view over Shek Kip
Mei, it's like you're in some European suburb."*

– Leumas To

17 Asia Art Archive
Map C, P.103

Born from a desire to preserve and celebrate
contemporary art in Asia, the Asia Art Archive
houses a collection of more than 50,000
records cataloguing important reference
material. The archive also hosts events including book displays, lecture series, art exhibitions
and workshops aimed at educating visitors and
providing a free-thinking environment for en-
gagement with art. Speak to one of the highly
knowledgeable librarians if you have questions
or wish to locate an item. Select publications
are available for purchase at the library.

🕙 1000–1800 (M–Sa except P.H.)
🏠 11F, Hollywood Ctr., 233 Hollywood Rd., Sheung Wan
📞 +852 2844 1112 🔗 www.aaa.org.hk

*"AAA has a really good art library with many books
and periodicals free for the public to read."*
– Studio TM

18 Sin Sin

Map C, P.103

Initiated by designer and entrepreneur Sin Sin Man, Sin Sin is one of the first galleries in Hong Kong to show Indonesian works and host exhibitions of artists from Southeast Asia, driving interest in and championing contemporary eastern art. Exhibitions are a mix of emerging and established artists and cross mediums from photography to canvas to sculpture. The gallery also hosts artist talks, and music and dance performances. Beside the gallery is Sin Sin Atelier, where you can buy handmade products by Sin Sin including purses, jewellery and clothing.

🕐 0930–1830 (M–Sa except P.H.)
🏠 52–54 Sai St., Sheung Wan
📞 Fine Art: +852 2858 5072, Atelier: +852 2521 0308
URL www.sinsin.com.hk

"*Sin Sin is the main push for Indonesian contemporary artists and broadens the public's taste. The gallery also actively supports community arts activities.*"

– Craig Au Yeung

19 Wontonmeen
Map L, P.108

Make no mistake, Wontonmeen is a "living room" meant to satisfy hunger for new ideas, rather than dumplings and noodles. Tucked into an old apartment building at the heart of Sham Shui Po, a district more known as a working class neighbourhood, this designer-run space summons artists and other curious of mind to converge at movie nights, workshops, mini concerts and art shows. Find upcycled furniture and installations made by Yuen Yeung, co-founder Patricia Choi's other venture.

🕐 1200-1600 daily
🏠 135 Lai Chi Kok Rd., Sham Shui Po
☎ +852 6904 0918
URL www.wontonmeen.com

"This is literally home to young creatives of varying disciplines. Besides the gallery, Wontonmeen also nestles a disc shop and have beds and bicycles for rent."

– Wong Ping

20 Above Second
Map C, P.102

Directed by May Wong, Above Second is a contemporary gallery space in up-and-coming Sai Ying Pun that shows local and international works. Exhibits range in style from pop art, street art, illustration, comic books and graphic design. Featuring fresh talents and focusing on an alternative sub-culture of graffiti and experimental works, the gallery aims to display modern, edgy creativity that other spaces may not show. There is no formula to their exhibitions – you may find small framed prints or wall-sized murals inside and outside the space.

🕐 1300–1900 (Tu–Sa)
🏠 9 First St., Sai Ying Pun   📞 +852 3483 7950
URL blog.above-second.com

"Speak with the friendly staff and ask them about the innovative projects that they get involved with."
– Used Pencil

21 Fringe Club
Map C, P.103

Virtually every day of the week, something exciting happens at the Fringe Club. Opened in 1984, in an old dairy farm depot, the club offers artists and performers a free space to showcase their work and collaborate with others on projects spanning multiple venues within the Fringe network. From bazaars and blues nights to live theatre and poetry reading, each space is designed to foster creative talent. Visit the Fringe Vault for an all-day breakfast in the surroundings of the former dairy's ice block, which still features original white tiled walls.

🕐 *1200 till late daily except P.H.*
🏠 *2 Lower Albert Rd., Central*
📞 *+852 2521 7251*　URL *www.hkfringeclub.com*

"The area (Lan Kwai Fong) is famous for drinking, clubbing and dining at the Fringe Club. Visitors can have a long night out after watching a show here."

– Gary Tong, TGIF

22 Broadway Cinematheque & Kubrick BC

Map I, P.106

Broadway Cinematheque showcases its cinematic devotion in multiple forms. Bookshop, café, gallery, disc store and art-house programmes can all be found at this one single venue. Dig into Cinegems for soundtracks, indie music and posters of international movies and animation. At Kubrick BC right next to the café, expect a rich selection of art zines, translated literature, cultural essays, local crafts, Kubrick publications and occasionally exhibitions and director talks.

🕐 *Kubrick BC: 1130–2200 daily* 🏠 *Prosperous Garden, 3 Public Square St., Yau Ma Tei* 📞 *+852 2388 0002, Kubrick BC: +852 2384 8929* URL *www. cinema.com.hk, www.kubrick.com.hk* 🔗 *Box office opens daily 30 mins before the first show*

"*Reserve more time for this place. Watch a movie and try their café.*"

– John Ho

23 Jao Tsung-I Academy
Map H, P.105

Named after the respected poet, calligrapher and scholar Jao Tsung-i, the institution runs extensive programmes on Chinese arts as well as Jao's lifelong pursuit. Topics span Chinese architecture, tea culture, visual arts, history and spiritual practices, in the form of retreats, exhibitions and short trips, where Jao's work is permanently on display at The Gallery (Low Zone). Perched on a hill above one of the city's first and largest private housing estates, the 32,000 square metre landscaped site belongs to a Grade III listed compound formerly served as a seaside customs station and health institution.

🕐 *0800–2200 daily*
🏠 *800 Castle Peak Rd., Lai Chi Kok*
📞 *+852 2100 2828* URL *www.jtia.hk*

"Ascend the hill to admire the breathtaking view of Mei Foo."

– Ah P, My Little Airport

24 Mapopo Community Farm
Map Q, P.110

Born as an endeavour to preserve their land in face of new development plans, Mapopo has grown into a citywide community united by sustainable living. Still an unrecognised village after 60 years, Ma Shi Po is destined to be wiped out after 2017. But third-generation villagers are striving to save their home, by boosting public interest in local farming, organic produce and by displaying art, putting on workshops and facilitating guided tours by one of them. Take exit A2 at Fanling MTR station for minibus 52A/56A to Wo Mun Street terminus, followed by a short walk. The entrance is marked by a blue letterbox.

🕐 Opening hours vary with programmes 🏠 Ma Sik Rd., Fanling
📞 +852 6121 8961
URL mapopo.wordpress.com

"They have farmer's market every Wednesday (2–6pm), and Sunday (11am–6pm), but always check for updates before departure."
– Kila Cheung

Markets & Shops

Vintage furniture, artisanal kitchenware and homemade dry goods

Hong Kong lives up to its name as a retail paradise with traditional and international goods streaming into the city. International brands have forced small independent shops to move upstairs or out of the urban metropolis and so old apartment buildings, industrial lodges and back alleyway premises house lesser-known wares waiting to be discovered. Be ready for a little adventure, which is also part of the fun.

In a city crazy for food, try and make homeware goods and local food your priorities. Visit Shanghai Street (#34) for kitchenware, steamers, ratten baskets and Chinese cake moulds; Des Voeux Road Central (#36) for homemade sauces and dried seafood products; and Island East Markets (*Tong Chong St., Tai Koo*) on Sundays handmade and sustainable goods. HK Honey, distributed online or at shops like Kapok (*3 Sun St., Wan Chai*), exemplifies the taste of urban bee farming in Hong Kong.

There are some quality vintage shops available in the city too, whether fashion items, second hand furniture or upcycled instruments. Pop into Select 18 & Mido Eyeglasses (#31), InBetween Shop (#28) or GrowthRing & Supply (#32) for menswear and vintage lifestyle products personally selected, designed or repaired. Chenmiji (#29) and Feelsogood (#27) stock curated furniture from various parts of the world.

Jacky Yu
Founder, Xi Yan

A designer-turned-chef, Yu opened Xi Yan in 2000 and published a couple of cookbooks. His signature recipes artistically blend the essence of Sichuan, Shanghai, Guangdong, Japanese, and Malay cuisines.

KniQ
P.053

Joey Ma
Fashion stylist

I have a passion for oil painting and styling, and I always encourage people to try different styles. Life is short, so let go of restrictions and enjoy life! Always be kind to others too!

Javin Mo
Founder, milkxhake

Mo is actively involved in collaborations with local and international clients from the arts, cultural and institutional sectors. He is also the creative director and design consultant of *Design 360°*.

PMQ
P.052

Feelsogood
Lifestyle
Store
P.054

Kinn Wong
Founder, InBetween Shop

Designer Wong owns a lifestyle shop and a graphic studio. He believes by bringing alternatives to the city that make it a better place to live in.

Chenmiji
P.058

Tommy Li
Founder, Tommy Li Design

Li belongs to the new generation of brand designers and consultants. Bold graphics, black humour and distinctive approaches are Li's signatures.

OBSCURA
THE ART OF DAILY LIFE

Obscura Magazine
Lifestyle magazine

Obscura Magazine cultivates the art of daily life. The printed and online journal collects and celebrates in small wonders and cherishes the remarkable beauty of creative minds.

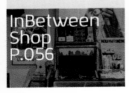

InBetween
Shop
P.056

Olympia
Graeco
Egyptian
Coffee
P.059

hehehe
Multimedia creative team

Formed in 2013, hehehe looks to inspire young independent minds. The trio is not afraid to challenge taboos and is committed to bringing the most cutting-edge and innovative elements to the scene.

Chris Cheung Hon-him
Founder, XEX & XCEED

Devoted to new media and interactive art, Cheung also produces music for TV commercials and films. He formed electronic duo VIM in 2008, XEX in 2007 and media art label XCEED in 2013.

Rayman Leung
Director, Fundamental Studio

Fundamental enhances corporate identity, print and web design through visual communication design based on substantial communication with clients.

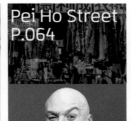

Central Saint Student
Blogger

An atypical beneficiary of HK's education system, he seeks to become expert in what he meets, speak up for injustice and satirise shameful acts. He always gives hope and at times curses the wicked.

Kylie Chan
Illustrator

Graduating in illustration from Camberwell College of Arts, Chan now draws for magazines. A great fan of zines, Chan's doing her best to save up for her very first own zine.

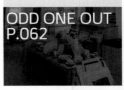

Peggy Chan
Founder, Grassroot Pantry & Prune

I founded GP and Prune with the aim to inspire and improve the health and wellness of the community through sustainably grown, local, organic food. Travelling inspires me, and creativity drives me.

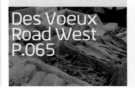

25 PMQ
Map C, P.103

Formerly the site of the Police Married Quarters, this vacant housing complex experienced a major change in 2010. The government looked to the creative industry to propose its preservation. The results have transformed the historic complex. Now home to more than 100 creatives, occupying converted dorm bunk units, PMQ is the hippest place to go to meet young creatives, and everything surrounding design. Besides shopping and spotting creatives at work, seek out D*Face's mural, and catch the art shows and night markets hosted by PMQ, individual studios or pop-up stores.

🕐 *Opening hours vary with studios*
🏠 *35 Aberdeen St., Central*
☎ *+852 2870 2335*
URL *www.pmq.org.hk*

"*Appreciate the 1950s architectural features well-repaired and maintained under the revitalisation scheme.*"

– Jacky Yu, Xi Yan

26 KniQ
Map E, P.104

For the latest, edgiest new fashion labels head to KNIQ, a boutique shop that carries women's, menswear and accessories from young emerging designers and known international fashion brands. The tucked away location is part of the experience of visiting the shop, which is coveted by local celebrities, and whose signatures you can find scribbled on the walls. Limited edition ranges and one off creations are common finds and command a hefty pricetag. Causeway Bay is a mecca for alternative fashion finds so explore nearby boutiques like Liger and Jexta.

🕐 1400–2200 (M–Sa), –2100 (Su)
🏠 4B, Vienna Mansion, 55 Paterson St., Causeway Bay
📞 +852 2881 7903
URL www.kniq.com.hk

"This is my favourite shop in Hong Kong for fashion! Make sure you find the right building."

– Joey Ma

27 Feelsogood Lifestyle Store
Map E, P.104

At a quiet corner of the emerging Tai Hang district lies an Art Deco building bursting hipster
vibes. It would be a shame if you pop in only
to check out their vintage lamp and light bulb
collections, since the Naked Sound Concert
normally plays Saturday evening at Feelsogood
Live upstairs, featuring instruments like san-
sula and handpan. To appreciate the full effect
of what this venue can offer, grab a reviving
brew from Unar Coffee just around the corner
and people watch. Chances are that you'll spot
a top model walking her petite Pekingese.

🏠 4 Second Ln., Tai Hang (at the
junction of Ormsby St. & Sherperd St.)
📞 +852 2865 6168
📘 Feelsogood lifestyle store

*"Find Feelsogood Live on second floor where mini
concerts and handicraft workshops take place.
It's closed on Mondays."*

– Javin Mo, milkxhake

28 InBetween Shop
Map C, P.103

Within its inviting blue shop front and quaint, quirky interiors, InBetween's founder Kinn Wong curates an eclectic mix of old and new objects. In addition to being full of curiosities such as one of a kind pottery mugs, antique weighing scales, movie posters and unique jewellery, the shop also hosts collaborations with artists to produce products, and workshops where you can make upcycled goods. Check out the market held on the last Sunday of each month. Tallensia is a floral art store next door where you can 'flowerjam'.

🕐 1200–1900 (Tu-Sa)
🏠 6B Tai Ping Shan St., Sheung Wan
📞 +852 9677 7815
URL inbetweenshop.com

"Our Sunday Market has a new theme each time. Don't miss this shop."

– Kinn Wong, InBetween Shop

29 Chenmiji
Map C, P.102

Skip checking what's nice and new at Chenmiji online, because owner Mike Chan cares more about his vintage furniture finds than reporting updates. Head to its new location on a Sheung Wan's back street, and you'll find yourself engulfed by classics like armchairs, chests and coffee tables by design champions like Arne Jacobsen and Eames. Chenmiji's second hand home decor and paraphernalia are personally sourced by Chan from Europe, repaired and spruced up for sale. Check out Chenmiji's self-published books!

🕐 1200-2000 daily 🏠 10 New St., Sheung Wan
📞 +852 2549 8800 🔗 www.chenmiji.com
🖇 Shop normally closes on Sundays

"A treasure trove for vintage lovers. Sift through their collections carefully. You'll always find gems in the pile."

– Tommy Li, Tommy Li Design Workshop

30 Olympia Graeco Egyptian Coffee

Map C, P.103

Olympia Graeco Egyptian Coffee is a long-standing business that started back in the 1930s. Critics claim that they serve the most perfectly roasted coffee beans in the city. Perhaps current owner and licensed Q Arabica Grader, Ms Ho can respond to that. Since an Egyptian trader opened it in 1927, this shop's priority has always been about using quality beans. Besides their daily roasts, you can also purchase authentic Turkish coffee tools and fresh beans at a low price. They know their beans well, and always roast them by hand.

🕙 1000–1900 (M–Sa except P.H.)
🏠 24 Old Bailey St., Central ☎ +852 2522 4653
f Olympia Graeco Egyptian Coffee

"Although it looks disordered and dingy, they sell top beans. It's definitely well worth a visit."

– Obscura Magazine

31 Select 18 & Mido Eyeglasses
Map C, P.103

Sharing the same space in a chic part of Sheung Wan, Select 18 and Mido house some of the best vintage finds in Hong Kong displayed in a chaotic, bohemian shop. Select 18 carries a range of luxury designer items, mostly accessories like handbags, hats and costume jewellery – pieces you won't find on the high street. Mido collection comprises over 20,000 vintage and contemporary glasses, sourced from around the world. There are frames for every face and budget. Try on several shapes to see what suits and don't be shy, ask for owner Mido's opinion.

🕐 1200–2100 (M–W),
–2300 (Th–Sa), –2000 (Su & PH)
🏠 18A Bridge St., Sheung Wan
☎ Select 18: +852 2858 8803, Mido:
+852 9121 3011 **f** midoeyeglasses

"Mido the shop owner is an encyclopaedia of vintage and contemporary eyewear and antiques (and bars!). Have your wallet and camera ready!"
– hehehe

32 GrowthRing & Supply
Map M, P.109

Call it a gallery, call it a warehouse. Anything that meets your eyes in this ample space is for sale. Opened in 2014 by Kenji Wong, former creative director of Wudai Shiguo, GrowthRing & Supply has done well for themselves, trading vintage furniture, apparel and lifestyle products. Revel in GRS' collection of unknown brands, local design and furnishings that Wong regularly acquires from places like Vietnam, India, Japan, and the States. Every so often you may come across a real exhibition of all things vintage!

🕐 1130–2030 (M-Sa) 🏠 5F, Block AB, How Ming Factory Bldg., 99 How Ming St., Kwun Tong 📞 +852 3462 3288 🔗 www.gr-supply.com

"They are not only a store. They are the story teller, telling and selling people thoughts and ideas."
– Rayman Leung, Fundamental Studio

33 ODD ONE OUT
Map D, P.104

Art is to be enjoyed here, whether you're an art maven or just nosy parker. Perched on the verge of Sau Wa Fong and St Francis Street in the happening Wan Chai neighbourhood, this art boutique and agency always seeks new global talent and artists, and hosts exhibitions showcasing highly characterful illustration. Works on display are often available for purchase as limited art prints, stationery and ceramics from as low as HK$50. ODD ONE OUT runs artist-led printmaking workshops too, so you can get involved!

🕐 1200–1930 daily 🏠 14 St Francis St., Wan Chai
📞 +852 2529 3955 URL oddoneout.hk

"This is a rare art space and boutique in Hong Kong solely dedicated to printed works. If you're looking for unique gifts and art zines, this is the place!"
– Kylie Chan

34 Shanghai Street
Map I, P.106

Lined with shops that cater to any commercial or domestic culinary needs, Shanghai Street sells every kitchen object imaginable from wooden mooncake moulds and bamboo streamers to pottery sake jugs and iron skillets, all affordably priced. Historically the street was one of Hong Kong's most bustling and prosperous. Architecture like the red brick listed building, site of an old pump house (344 Shanghai St.) and market vendors drying fish and fruit the traditional way almost transports you back in time.

🕐 Opening hours vary with shops
🏠 Yau Ma Tei

"*Go casual. Sneakers are recommended, as it's always wet.*"

– Chris Cheung Hon-him, XEX & XCEED

35 Pei Ho Street
Map L, P.108

Streets have developed their own character in this culturally textured old district. Home to a local grassroots community, Sham Shui Po is your place for affordable finds. Reserve a day to explore the area, starting from the noisy and messy Pei Ho Street, which sells HK$20 sneakers, tools, street food and curios. Trading continues well into witching hour and it's fun to go late. Don't miss out the famous Apliu Street for second-hand electronics, Yu Chau Street for fabrics and beads and, across Cheung Sha Wan Road, Fok Wing Street for Toys. Bring a torch to hunt for treasures at the night market!

🏠 *Sham Shui Po*   🖉 *Cash only*

"It never disappoints when you want to see another side of this cosmopolitan metropolis."

– Central Saint Student

36 Des Voeux Road West

Map C, P.102

Take a stroll down Des Voeux Road West and overwhelm your senses with the whiff of dried food, from salted fish and dried mushrooms to orange peel. Fish are strung upside down and hang from shop fronts, and deep bins are packed full of dried fruits sold in bulk. Used in both cooking and health tonics, dried seafood is an important staple in the Chinese diet. Sample shredded spiced cuttlefish, a popular snack, and fuel up on nuts and other nibbles.

🏠 *Sheung Wan*

"Find yourself immersed within the scents of dried scallops and the sights of sun-dried sea cucumbers on traditional bamboo straw trays."

– Peggy Chan, Grassroot Pantry & Prune

Restaurants & Cafés

Knock-out Cantonese cuisine, artistic desserts and sustainable eats

The food scene is much like the character of this city: busy and eventful. Hongkongers work hard for each tasty treat and delight in each choice – and choices are endless. From regional Chinese cuisine to Japanese delicacies and South Asian fare, both authentic home cooking and newer innovations tempt the palate.

If you're on the street with an empty stomach in the early hours, go to Tai Kok Tsui (Ivy St.), Jordan (Ferry St.), Sai Wan Ho, Tin Hau (Electric Rd.) and Causeway Bay (Jardin St., Cannon St., Yiu Wah St.) and feast on Teochew cuisine or Cantonese desserts. But call Tsui Wah (*www.tsuiwahdelivery.com*) instead, if you crave local favourites delivered to your door.

While many restaurants and cafés remain focused on traditional cooking, and hold sentimental meaning for customers, others reinterpret and reinvent and break new boundaries. You can't leave Hong Kong without trying Guangdong cuisine. Dim sum (#40, #47), and wok-fries (#48), barbecue roast (#37), cured meat, hot pot, clay pot rice (#58) and dessert soups (#56) all deserve sampling. An increased awareness of health and well-being has given rise to new sustainable eating habits and a balanced diet. Make a booking at O-Veg (#42) to experience a clean and ethical eat.

Adonian Chan
Graphic designer & musician

HKPolyU graduate Chan co-founded design outfit TRI-LINGUA in 2010 and the cultural and dining space Syut with his band tfvsjs in 2014. Chan has been researching Wei Dynasty engraving since 2011.

Yung Kee Restaurant P.070

Goldfinch Restaurant P.071

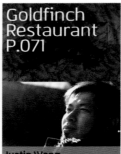

Justin Wong
Comic & media artist

Critical of social affairs and politics, Wong's cartoons and illustrations have been featured in multiple local newspapers and magazines. Wong also teaches at the Hong Kong Baptist university.

Michael Leung
Designer & urban farmer

Leung focuses on socio-cultural and environmental projects in HK. His work ranges from conceptual objects for the diseased to urban agriculture projects such as HK Honey and HK Farm.

Mido Café P.072

Joyce Wang
Founder, Joyce Wang Studio

I specialise in hospitality and residential design. My first job was done with a friend and was the cabana rooms of LA's Roosevelt Hotel. My portfolio also includes AMMO Restaurant & Bar and Mott 32 in Hong Kong.

Mott 32 P.073

Syut P.074

Anson Mak
Video & sound artist, educator

Mak explores film and video art in terms of experimental ethnography, digital communities, and the novelty of using super 8 film in the digital era. She's also a vegetarian hoping for more compassion in all beings.

Chock Ma
Band

Chok Ma voices their beliefs through a blend of post rock and heavy metal, on top of traditional Chinese music and Buddhism-inspired lyrics where energy and cultures clash.

O-Veg P.076

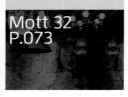

Jianchi Chen
Designer, thecaveworkshop

Chen co-founded thecave-workshop in 2010. Having been involved in various art and design creations, the cave now focuses on experimental product design for living.

ATUM Desserant P.078

Ivan Yu
Founder, OFFTHEHABIT

Born in Hong Kong, Yu is a film director and OFFTHEHABIT's founder, which specialises in commercials and music videos.

LAAB
Design studio

Co-founded by Hang Yip, Ricci Wong, Otto Ng and Geoff Chan, LAAB develops progressive designs through technology and craftsmanship. LAAB's work ranges between "Art" and "Architecture".

Mavericks P.077

For Kee Restaurant P.080

Chochukmo
Band

Chochukmo belongs to no category. Their music is dynamic and playful, as individuals of the five-piece group contribute their own understanding to define experimental rock.

DimDimSum Dim Sum Specialty Store P.082

Six Lee
Founder, SixLee

Lee graduated from the Royal Academy of Fine Arts Antwerpen in 2009 before joining Alexander McQueen's menswear team. SixLee stresses unique silhouettes derived from traditional British tailoring and mannish details.

Jay Forster
Founding partner, Clockenflap

I am the artistic director of Clockenflap Music and Arts Festival. I have lived and worked in Hong Kong for 18 years and consider this my home.

Chungking Mansions P.081

Java Road Cooked Food Centre P.083

37 Yung Kee Restaurant
Map C, P.103

Yung Kee's lustrous façade is the epitome of its family tradition and culinary achievements. Beginning as a modest cooked food stall in the 1930s, the late founder Kam Shui-fai turned his venture into a legend fare like *wonton*, *pidan* (preserved eggs), and Cantonese barbecue – though rumour has it that the real first-rate plates are reserved only for VIPs. The restaurant's large logotype is a fine sample of Hong Kong store sign calligraphy and is an engraving type that originated in the Wei Dynasty. Later it was refined by masters Zhao Zhi-qian (1829–84) and Au Kin-kung (1887–1971).

🕐 1100–2330 daily
🏠 32–40 Wellington St., Central
📞 +852 2522 1624
🔗 www.yungkee.com.hk

"Yung Kee's roast goose is the only reason you need."
– Adonian Chan

38 Goldfinch Restaurant
Map E, P.104

From the vintage decor to the gentle whiff of fatty steaks on sizzling cast iron skillets, Goldfinch evokes nostalgia for Hong Kong's good old days. The dimly-lit steakhouse has been interpreting its own idea of western cuisine since the 1960s – and is quite stuck there. An odd range of grilled and roast meats and fish runs the gauntlet from beef and spring lamb to baby pigeon, ostrich, grilled lobster and whole abalone. The decor is drenched in nostalgia, giving a flavour of what visitors to Hong Kong decades ago would have discovered. If set menus at HK$130-230 exceed your budget, come for their "tea sets" starting from HK$43.

🕐 1100-2330 daily
🏠 13-15 Lan Fong Rd., Causeway Bay
📞 +852 2577 7981

"A favourite filming location for director Wong Ka-wai, and one of the few surviving restaurants serving Hong Kong-style "western" steaks. Ask for baked pork chop rice."

– Justin Wong

071

39 Mido Café
Map I, P.106

Hongkongers, especially the working classes' desire for affordable enjoyment during the colonial era is encapsulated in Mido's authentic 1950s decoration and old-school westernised menu. Occupying the bottom floors of a postwar tenement house with a beautiful curved front, this family-run café dishes out classic Cantonese comfort food, ranging from fried noodles, rice dishes in any number of combinations of ready-made sauce and meat, to sandwiches and toast best paired with milk tea. Come between lunch and dinner for a possible moment of peace.

🕐 1000-2100 daily
🏠 63 Temple St., Yau Ma Tei

"When the sun sets, sit by the window and enjoy that moment when the cafe staff turn on the beautiful neon sign outside."
– Michael Leung

 Mott 32
Map C, P.103

"Exquisite" sums up both the modern Chinese fare and Joyce Wang's interiors at this swanky restaurant. Previously helming the Michelin-starred Dynasty Restaurant at the Renaissance Hotel, Mott 32's acclaimed chef, Fung Man-yip masters traditional Cantonese dishes with upscale ingredients and equipment. Wallow in their inspired presentation. *Siu mai* consisting soft-boiled quail eggs and Kurobuta pork, tea-infused cocktails and soy-sauce ice-cream are one-of-a-kind design delicacies.

🕐 *1200–0000 daily* 🏠 *Standard Chartered Bank Bldg., 4–4a Des Voeux Rd. C., Central*
📞 *+852 2885 8688* URL *www.mott32.com*
🔗 *Bookings required*

"Book a table in the Tangerine Room!"

– Joyce Wang, Joyce Wang Studio

41 Syut
Map M, P.109

The local band tfvsjs' prime business is indubitably music, but this 370 square metre venture proves the rockers also have a passion for cooking, motion picture and design. Playing host to underground film screenings and talks every so often, Syut also doles out killer dishes six days a week, expertly prepared by chef and bass guitarist Pang. With views over the area's semi-functioning industrial village, make yourself comfortable in this warehouse and talk to the band members at the bar or their built-in studio. Cured fish and vegetarian salad make for an appetising start.

🕐 1830–2200 (M), 1200–1500, 1830–2200 (Tu–Sa)
🏠 10B, Gee Luen Factory Bldg., 316–318 Kwun Tong Rd., Kwun Tong (Entrance on Tai Yip St)
📞 +852 2415 4999 ⓕ tfvsjs.syut

"Don't miss the sunset over the now defunct Kai Tak Airport in Kowloon Bay."

– Anson Mak

42 O-Veg

Map O, P.109

A truthful commitment to naturalist urban life-style, O-Veg opens only on Fridays and week-ends to serve what's freshly picked from their on-site organic farm. A staunch advocate of sustainable living, owner Steve Cheung channels what he learnt from veteran eco-activists and trips to rural villages around the world into his life and food. A basic three-course meal costs about HK$200, with main draws the freshmade bread and pizzas. Buddhist and raw vegan meals are available on request.

🕐 1830–2230 (F–Su), 1130–1430 (Sa–Su, Oct–Feb)
🏠 53 Tai Kwong Po Village, Kam Tin
📞 +852 2893 3037 f O-Veg
✎ Cash only, Make bookings 2 weeks ahead

"O-Veg's location is a tricky one. Be sure you check the route before setting off and look up on the way to admire the beautiful New Territories scenery."

– Chock Ma

43 Mavericks

Map P, P.110

Conceived by chef Austin Fry and art director Jay FC, this bar, restaurant and surf shack is the ultimate destination for great views and food. Maverick's strong mission to support smaller food producers means its western style menu features micro breweries, locally caught fish and breads made at a nearby bakery. They also make their own sausages, grow a herb garden and recycle their food waste. Indulge in tenderloin stuffed with fried oysters smothered with béarnaise sauce for a main and round it off with an artisan ice pop. Admire the driftwood furniture and artworks, all made by local artists and designers.

🕐 1700–2330 (F), 1100– (Sa–Su & P.H.)
🏠 Pui O Beach, Lantau Island
+852 5662 8552
f Mavericks HK

"Mavericks also serves veggie and children's menus. Bring your swimming suit and go bask in the sun. They have surfboards for rent!"
– Jianchi Chen, thecaveworkshop

44 ATUM Desserant

Map E, P.104

Just opened in 2014, this "dessert-aurant" offers culinary experiments and spectacles in textures, flavours and perceptions. It is most known for its 'Improvisation', as the founders and chefs paint and assemble what looks like abstract art on a silicon canvas right before your eyes. Ingredients include jelly, mouse, meringues, ice-cream, crisps, honeycomb toffee, matcha and cakes among other sweet sensations, where the 'painting' is almost too good to eat. Other than improvisation, they also offer a seasonal menu that contains eight different plates.

🕐 1300-0000 (Tu-Su)　🏠 16F, The L.Square, 459-461 Lockhart Rd., Causeway Bay　📞 +852 2956 1411
📘 ATUM Desserant

"Experimental dessert-making as a performing art."
– LAAB

45 For Kee Restaurant
Map C, P.103

At the rim of this hipster district near Soho stands a modest, time-honoured tea restaurant with experienced staff adamant about cooking at their own pace. The reason is obvious once you champ down on their masterly fried pork chops, or their ultra thick toast stuffed with sauté beef and onions in satay sauce. Feel free to top up your plate with vegetables, braised mushrooms, or eggs. For

Kee's milk tea and coffee is a must have for regulars, but request it sugar free if you don't have much of a sweet tooth. The place often fills to capacity and customers are often asked to share tables with strangers.

🕐 0700–1630 (M–F), 0700–1530 (Sa)
🏠 200 Hollywood Rd., Soho
📞 +852 2546 8947   🖉 Cash only

"You won't find glamorous decor, and it takes patience to get seated due to limited capacity. Ask for rice with pork chop and egg, or a beef satay sandwich!"

– Ivan Yu, OFFTHEHABIT

46 Chungking Mansions
Map G, P.105

Experience a red carpet walk as you approach Chungking Mansions with restaurant promoters and knockoff touts chasing you down Nathan Road. Once a filming location of Wong Ka-wai's *ChungKing Express* (1994), the five-block establishment is now better known as a home away from home for South-Asian communities, and a food haven for local foodies. Go down the passageways from the main entrance to reach the lift and the floor directory. Khyber Pass on the 7th floor has earned the most hype, mostly through word of mouth.

🕐 Opening hours vary with restaurants
🏠 36–44 Nathan Rd., Tsim Sha Tsui
URL www.chungkingmansions.com.hk

"It's true as people say – always keep an eye out for your wallet – you could go broke for the food!"

– Chochukmo

47 DimDimSum Dim Sum Specialty Store

Map I, P.106

DimDimSum is a land of dim sums where you can find classic dishes with a modern twist. There's also an impressive dim sum range made with vegetarian-only and medicinal ingredients. The unconventional menu offers adventurous flavour combinations, including pan-fried wasabi stuffed dumplings and *xiaolongbao* with black truffle, at reasonable prices. Try crispy steamed rice noodle rolls for an alternative texture and their pineapple bun for an intriguing take on the traditionally fruit-free bun.

🕐 1000-0100 daily 🏠 21–23 Man Ying St., Jordan
📞 +852 2771 7766 📘 DimDimSum Dim Sum Specialty Store 🔗 This spot has 4 locations, each with varying business hours

"I would say this is the best place to have contemporary dim sum."

– Six Lee, SixLee

48 Java Road Cooked Food Centre

Map F, P.105

Divided up by multiple restaurants each specialising in a Chinese regional cuisine, this neighbourhood spot is perpetually packed and requires a wait. Sichuan, Teochew and Cantonese cuisine ranging from nutritious congees to fingerlicking *dai pai dong*-style stir-fries are at your fingertips, however cross-kitchen ordering is impossible so pick a kitchen before you seat yourself. Tung Po is arguably the most popular stall on site. Go and appreciate their unique workplace and foodie interpretations of various traditions and cultures. The buzz and frivolity are part of the lure.

🕐 1730–0030 daily 🏠 99 Java Rd., North Point
📞 Tung Po: +852 2880 5224 📎 Cash only, reservation required for selected dishes at Tung Po

"As is often the case in Hong Kong, a sterile food court has been claimed back by the local restaurateurs. Be bold – order the unfamiliar."
– Jay Forster, Clockenflap

Nightlife

Soul soothing hikes, night markets and more adventurous eats

Unsurprisingly this sparkly city has something for every taste. At night Hong Kong is ever shifting. Sharing a great love for fun and the city, young (and young-at-heart) creatives continually define and redefine the place they call home. The club scene remains an essential part of the picture, but peace is also what some are after in this restless city. An edgy mix of art, attitude, sounds and light make this place unpredictable and engrossing for outsiders and its inhabitants day and night.

Get in touch with regional music at one of the privately-run live music venues dotted around the city. Hidden Agenda (#54) and jazz bars like Visage One (*93 Hollywood Rd., Central*) and Peel Fresco (*49 Peel St., Central*) should definitely go on your list. Also, watch out for young artists trying to reclaim public space in Causeway Bay and Tsim Sha Tsui.

Home to more than 1,200 skyscrapers, the vertical city boasts one of the world's most stunning skylines. Although their lights fade to black after 11pm, there's plenty of time to enjoy this mesmerising night vista through activities such as night hiking, ferry riding, and sifting goods on neon-clad streets at a night market. If you are keen on visiting a night market, try the unofficial market on Pei Ho Street (#35), but bring a torch if you want to rummage. Hong Kong's inexpensive taxis and comprehensive public transport system enables nights out a safe return from even the wildest nights.

Alexis Holm
Founder, squarestreet

Originally from Stockholm, I've been calling HK home for five years now. I'm a fashion designer by trade, but also run a small fashion boutique, "squarestreet" at 15 Square St., in Sheung Wan.

The Pawn
P.089

Above Second
Art gallery

Above Second focuses on urban contemporary art. This includes the best of street art and murals brought in by Director May Wong and gallery manager Lauren Every-Wortman.

Brainrental
Creative trio

Brainrental blends the humour and absurdities of modern city life to create wonder for all to ponder. The creative trio's focuses span illustration, murals, and lifestyle products.

Yardbird
P.088

Yardbird

Bibo
P.090

STYLO VISION
Creative agency

Founder and creative director Thomas Lee and director/producer Andrew Lang form STYLO VISION. They tell brand stories through innovative visual campaigns.

Ping Pong
129 乒乓體
P.092

Raymond Lee & Amber Fu
Founders, RMM

RMM is Readymade Magazine and RMM Journal, two platforms where the creative duo shares stories with readers. Positivity and the mission to inspire propel RMM's work.

Graphicairlines
Creative duo

"Cute, we are not." Homegrown artists Tat and Vi celebrates the beauty of ugliness. GraphicAirlines remark on a city's material life and distending desires.

001
P.091

Hidden
Agenda
P.094

Ben McCarthy
Creative director, Charlie & Rose

I was born and bred in Australia and have spent many years working in Europe and Asia. I always search for the best places to eat, the weirdest spots to drink and the most incredible outdoor areas to explore.

Missy Ho's
P.095

Yuen Kee
Dessert
Specialist
P.096

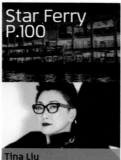

David Yeung
Co-founder, Green Monday

An active green living promoter, Yeung is named The Purpose Economy 100 Asia, "Local Heros", and "Men of the Year" by magazines. Green Monday was "Idea of the Year".

C&G Artpartment
Creative space

C&G Artpartment is by Clara Cheung and Gum Cheng. Founded in 2007, the space uses art to respond to social and cultural issues. C&G also pay close attention to art ecology in HK.

Night Hikes
P.097

Kay Wong
Co-founder, Daydream Nation

Creator and chef designer of fashion arts house, Daydream Nation. DN's clothes come as a reaction to the strong racism against daydreamers in the city.

Temple
Street
P.098

Star Ferry
P.100

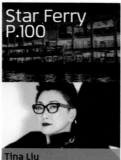

Tina Liu
Fashion stylist

With experiences in the film, television, radio, music, stage, publishing and fashion, Liu's fortes are many. Tina's Choice is her latest venture since 2013.

Rex Koo
Graphic designer

Born and bred in HK, Koo began "Simple People" in 2013. His exhibitions and related products have won tremendous acclaim.

Neon Sign
Tour
P.101

49 Yardbird

Map C, P.103

The hardest decision of the evening at Yardbird will be whether to drink whisky, sake, shochu or all three. With that decision made get stuck into the plates of moorish crowd pleasers: sweet corn tempura or KFC – Korean fried cauliflower are signatures. Since they take no booking, show up before 6.20pm if you want to secure a table at the Yakatori eatery and bar designed by Dix Design and architecture.

Proprietors Matt Abergel and Lindsay Jang also own Ronin on nearby On Wo Lane, if you just can't get enough of their food.

🕐 0600–0000 (M-Sa)
🏠 33 Bridge St., Sheung Wan ☎ +852 2547 9273
🔗 www.yardbirdrestaurant.com

"Go for dinner or just hang out at the bar having a drink. They specialise in chicken done the Japanese way, but there's more to it than poultry."

– Alexis Holm, squarestreet

50 The Pawn

Map D, P.104

Experience eclectic British charm at this former pawn shop set in a 19th century four-storey heritage building. Designed by restaurant co-founder Alan Lo, with artworks curated by local artist Stanley Wong, the variety of areas offer atmospheres that cater to everyone. The first floor houses 'Botanicals', a bar offering cocktail creations that draw on unusual herbs, spices and taste pairings. On the second floor, 'Kitchen' serves unique modern British cuisine made under the culinary direction of Michelin-starred chef, Tom Aikens. Early birds may want to give lifestyle store Tang Tang Tang Tang underneath a look-see.

🕐 1200–0100 (Su-Th), –0200 (F-Sa)
🏠 62 Johnston Rd., Wan Chai 📞 +852 2866 3444
URL www.thepawn.com.hk

"Go for afternoon tea or a nice evening cocktail and make sure to sit out on the porch if the weather's nice!"

– Above Second

51 Bibo
Map C, P.103

Bibo is its own masterpiece, full of art and wall murals by trendy contemporary artists including Banksy, Basquiat and Murakami, the restaurant serves fine French cuisine, and creative cocktails are expertly made by a team of mixologists using quality ingredients, sparing no expense. Try "Viva la Revolucion" for interesting flavours or enjoy Absinthe presented the traditional way, with ice-cold water poured from a fountain, over sugar. The street itself has much to offer, explore the many actual galleries and bars nearby.

🕐 1200-1430, 1830-0000 (M-F),
1130-1530, 1830-0000 (Sa-Su)
🏠 163 Hollywood Rd., Sheung Wan
📞 +852 2956 3188 ⓕ Bibo

"Paintings and sculptures are scattered throughout the space. Remember to look around while you're catching up with your friends, something will amaze you."
– Brainrental

52 001

Map C, P.103

Behind an unmarked black door behind the closed green hawker booths, this clandestine speakeasy is designed to be found only by those in the know. With its sultry jazz, velvet upholstery and ambient lighting, an elegant and intimate environment is set for visitors keen to be transported back in time. Savour top notch, forbidden cocktails. The earl grey martini is a must. If you're feeling peckish there are a variety of nibbles on offer, like grilled cheese and fried chicken.

🕐 1800–0100 (M–F), –0200 (Th–Sa)
🏠 Basement, Welley Bldg., 97 Wellington St., Central (Entrance on Graham St.) 📞 +852 2810 6969

> *"Famous speakeasy – oxymoron! Live jazz Tuesday nights starts at 9.30pm. No bookings, so be there earlier. Pricey, but you get what you pay for."*
>
> – STYLO VISION

53 Ping Pong 129
Map C, P.102

Arguably the first proper Spanish gin and tonic bar in Hong Kong, Ping Pong has more than an exceptional gin selection to please local hipsters. Situated in an ex-table tennis hall, the lofty space has a vast ceiling and oozes a vibe just co-owner Juan Martínez Gregorio has always wanted. A wall of local artists' work occupies your gaze as you sample unusual gins and botanicals poured over hand-cut ice. A fave place for private parties and pop-up functions, it pays to check their agenda before you go.

🕐 1800-late (Tu-Sa), -0000 (Su)
🏠 129 Second St., Sai Ying Pun
📞 +852 9158 1584 **f** Ping Pong 129

"This place does the best gin in Hong Kong."
– Raymond Lee & Amber Fu, RMM

54 Hidden Agenda
Map M, P.109

Hidden Agenda (HA) is both a beacon to and a cradle for Hong Kong's independent music scene. Opened by young music buffs in 2009, the live house invites homegrown and regional talents to rock the stage, with a whole spectrum of music from reggae to experimental and post rock. Previous guests to grace the stage are Tahiti 80, 65daysofstatic, JJ and How To Dress Well taking HA as their Asia tour Hong Kong stops. With a capacity of just 300, be sure you keep a close eye on their programmes and grab your tickets fast. Bring your own drink and be ready to go crazy and get gritty!

🕐 Ⓢ Showtime & ticket price vary with programmes 🏠 2A, Winful Industrial Bldg., 15-17 Tai Yip St., Kwun Tong 📞 +852 9088 8950
🔗 hiddenagenda.hk

"It's an indie gem in the deepest part of Kowloon."
– Graphicairlines

55 Missy Ho's
Map A, P.102

An eccentric mix of birdcages, kitschy vases and art adorn the interior of Missy Ho's, located next to K-Town bar & grill in up-and-coming Kennedy Town. Cocktails are carefully crafted using a combination of unexpected flavours, tweaking modern classics. Bloody Mr. Ho is a Bloody Mary with rum and beer replacing the traditional vodka base. Each creation is garnished elegantly for a touch of visual intrigue. Arrive early and try the amazing Pan-Asian, and Mexican fusion food before getting your grove on.

🕐 1800-2300 (M-Sa) 🏠 Shop G9, Sincere Western Hse., 48 Forbes St., Kennedy Town
📞 +852 2817 3808 📘 Missy Ho's

"Dress like a monkey but try not to kill yourself on the swings. I'd be surprised if you can remember what you ate since the cocktails are bottomless!"
– Ben McCarthy, Charlie & Rose

56 Yuen Kee Dessert Specialist
Map C, P.102

Yuen Kee has been serving traditional Chinese dessert soups for as long as locals can remember. Their speciality is their tried-and-tested recipe for *sang jì sheng cha*, a clear "tea" made with the twig of viscum album and dried longan, best paired with boiled egg and lotus seeds. A couple of their most popular choices are ground walnut, almond, black sesame, and the red or green bean soups, as well as steamed custard and sponge cakes. Despite their sugary content, Chinese dessert soups generally are health-giving and curative for fatigue. Hot desserts give maximum nutritive value.

🕐 1200–2330 daily 🏠 32 Centre St., Western District ☎ +852 2548 8687

"Chinese dessert soup was what I missed most while studying abroad. Yuen Kee's black sesame soup and sang jì sheng cha are recommended."

– David Yeung, Green Monday

Seek a brief respite from the frenetic streets and overwhelming heat in the summer with a night hike. High Island Reservoir East Dam really delivers something out of ordinary. Visit this geological site in the late afternoon to view hexagonal volcanic tuffs, stacked islands, and a breathtaking sunset above the Pacific Ocean. As day gives way to night, stars can be glimpsed – an elusive sight given Hong Kong's severe light pollution. The only way to access and leave the East Dam is by taxi. Wait for one at the roundabout by the green-roofed pavilion, or use a smartphone app to summon one when you're ready to leave.

🏠 *Sai Kung Man Yee Rd., Sai Kung*
🔗 *www.geopark.gov.hk/en_s4f7.htm*

"Total darkness descends outside of the city's glare. In principal, it's safe to hike at night, but you can always go in a group and count on a friend or two."

– C&G Artpartment

58 Temple Street
Map I, P.106

The vendors shouts and neighbourhood din on Temple Street stay true to the essence of old Hong Kong. Stretching across Jordan and Yau Ma Tei, the area comes to life at night, when palm readers and hawkers set up their stalls displaying all kinds of knick-knacks from novelty lighters, gadgets, souvenirs, and jade to sex toys. But don't just linger at the market. At the Yau Ma Tei section restaurants are tucked behind the stalls, but spill onto the streets for a back-to-basics Al Fresco experience. Stir-fries, sizzling clay pot rice and cold beers are orders of the day and night.

🏠 *From Jordan Rd. to Yau Ma Tei*

"Always bargain at the market stalls. There are very old fashioned dance floors where you can order food from outside. Have tea or beer and dance along."
– Kay Wong, Daydream Nation

 59 Star Ferry
Map G, P.105

Locals and tourists all agree that viewing dazzling Victoria Harbour at night never gets old. Brightly lit LED sign boards and the city's most expensive real estates are all included in this beautiful panoramic view. Tsim Sha Tsui Pier is the last remaining to display an original 1950 façade and can be viewed alongside the King of Kowloon's (1921-2007) calligraphy-style graffiti and a 1915 clock tower on the nearby promenade. Only the Central route opens its lower deck to offer the dim light and diesel fumes experienced by the ferry's first riders. Watch signs to locate the right entrance for respective decks and routes.

🕐 Central Route (CR): 0630–2330 daily, Wan Chai route (WCR): 0720–2250 daily 🅢 $2.5/1.5 (M–F), $3.4/2.1 (Sa–Su & P.H.), CR lower deck: $2/1.4 (M–F), $2.8/2 (Sa–Su & P.H.) 🌐 www.starferry.com.hk

"If one can help it, opt out of an air conditioned cabin. Experience the natural breezes. Though humid and hot in the Summer months that IS real Hong Kong."
– Tina Liu

60 Neon Sign Tour

The red, yellow, green and cyan neon signs energise busy streets after dark. Hung outside old Chinese karaoke clubs, restaurants, pawn shops, mahjong parlours and jewellers, these signposts come in all sorts of shapes and sizes. The best time to view the sea of original neon signs is now, as safety regulations, cheap banners and LED boards are driving them off the streets. Take a bus from Sham Shui Po to Tsim Sha Tsui, or a tram from North Point to Western District to be dazzled. Front seats on the upper deck offer the best vantage point.

URL Neon map: www.neonsigns.hk

"Besides night views on both sides of Victoria Harbour, neon signs blinking against the dark sky has to be one of Hong Kong's most iconic images."

– Rex Koo

DISTRICT MAPS : **KENNEDY TOWN, HAPPY VALLEY**

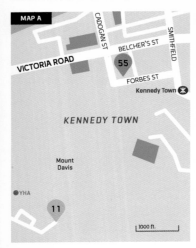

MAP A

CADOGAN ST
SMITHFIELD
BELCHER'S ST
VICTORIA ROAD
55
FORBES ST
Kennedy Town ✴

KENNEDY TOWN

Mount
Davis

● YHA

11

1000 ft.

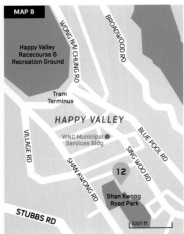

MAP B

WONG NAI CHUNG RD
BROADWOOD RD
Happy Valley
Racecourse &
Recreation Ground

Tram
Terminus

HAPPY VALLEY

VILLAGE RD
WNC Municipal ●
Services Bldg
SHAN KWONG RD
BLUE POOL RD
SING WOO RD
12
Shan Kwong
Road Park
STUBBS RD

1000 ft.

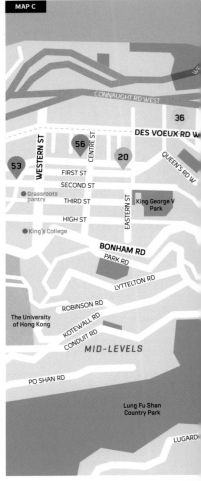

MAP C

CONNAUGHT RD WEST

36

DES VOEUX RD W

WESTERN ST
56
CENTRE ST
20
QUEEN'S RD W
53
FIRST ST
SECOND ST
● Grassroots
pantry
THIRD ST
EASTERN ST
King George V
Park
HIGH ST

● King's College

BONHAM RD
PARK RD

LYTTELTON RD

ROBINSON RD

The University
of Hong Kong
KOTEWALL RD
CONDUIT RD
MID-LEVELS

PO SHAN RD

Lung Fu Shan
Country Park

LUGARD

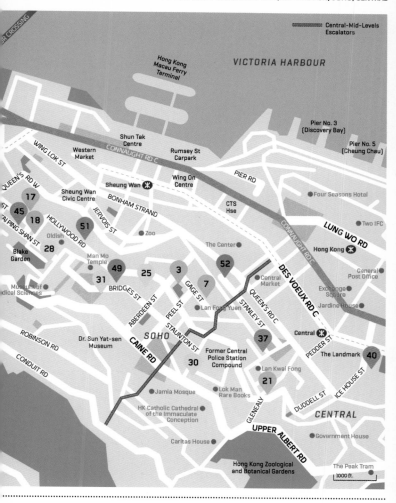

- 31_Select 18 & Mido Eyeglasses
- 36_Des Voeux Road West
- 37_Yung Kee Restaurant
- 40_Mott 32
- 45_For Kee Restaurant
- 49_Yardbird
- 51_Bibo
- 52_001
- 53_Ping Pong 129
- 55_Missy Ho's
- 56_Yuen Kee Dessert Specialist

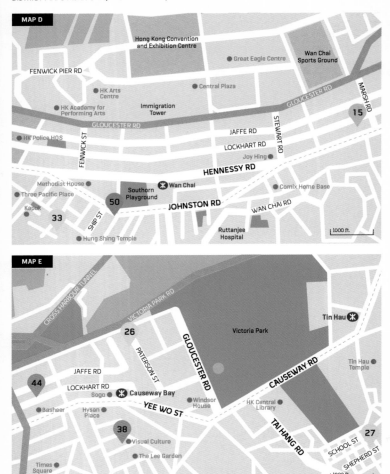

- ● 15_Art & Cultural Outreach
- ● 26_KniQ
- ● 27_Feelsogood Lifestyle Store
- ● 33_ODD ONE OUT
- ● 38_Goldfinch Restaurant
- ● 44_ATUM Desserant
- ● 50_The Pawn

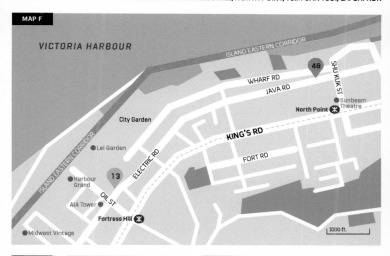

MAP F

VICTORIA HARBOUR

ISLAND EASTERN CORRIDOR

48 · SHU KUK ST.

WHARF RD

JAVA RD

Sunbeam Theatre

North Point ✳

City Garden

KING'S RD

ISLAND EASTERN CORRIDOR

Lei Garden

ELECTRIC RD

13

FORT RD

Harbour Grand

OIL ST

AIA Tower

Fortress Hill ✳

Midwest Vintage

1000 ft.

MAP G

Kowloon Park

Kowloon Mosque and Islamic Centre

HAIPHONG RD

TSIM SHA TSUI · Tsim Sha Tsui ✳

46

ISQUARE

CANTON RD

KOWLOON PARK DR

NATHAN RD

Harbour City

1881 Heritage

The Peninsula

SALISBURY RD

59

HK Space Museum

Hong Kong Cultural Centre

Hong Kong Museum of Art

Avenue of Stars

VICTORIA HABOUR

1000 ft.

MAP H

CASTLE PEAK RD

✳ Mei Foo (B)

23

Mei Foo Bus Terminus

KWAI CHUNG RD

LAI CHI KOK RD

Mei Foo Sun Chuen

Lai Chi Kok Park

W KOWLOON HIGHWAY

1000 ft.

- 13_I'mperfect Xchange@Oil
- 23_Jao Tsung-I Academy
- 46_Chungking Mansions
- 48_Java Road Cooked Food Centre
- 59_Star Ferry

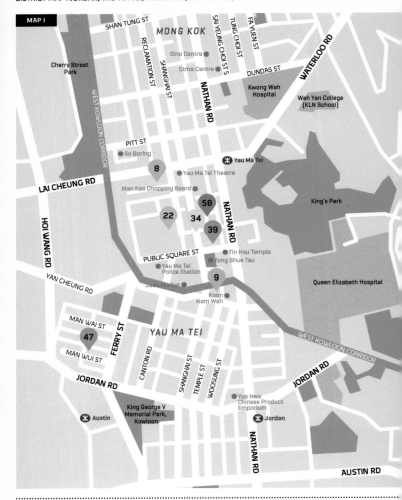

- 8_Yau Ma Tei Wholesale Fruit Market
- 9_Yau Ma Tei Carpark Building
- 22_Broadway Cinematheque & Kubrick BC
- 34_Shanghai Street
- 39_Mido Café
- 47_DimDimSum Dim Sum Specialty Store
- 58_Temple Street

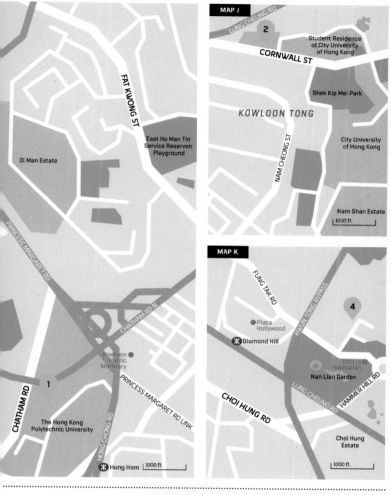

MAP J

LUNG CHEUNG RD

2

Student Residence
of City University
of Hong Kong

CORNWALL ST

Shek Kip Mei Park

KOWLOON TONG

NAM CHEONG ST

City University
of Hong Kong

East Ho Man Tin
Service Reservoir
Playground

FAT KWONG ST

Oi Man Estate

Nam Shan Estate

1000 ft.

MAP K

PRINCESS MARGARET RD

FUNG TAK RD

KWUN TONG BYPASS

4

Plaza
Hollywood

CHATHAM RD N

Diamond Hill

Chi Lin
Vegetarian

Nan Lian Garden

LUNG CHEUNG RD

HAMMER HILL RD

PRINCESS MARGARET RD LINK

Kowloon
Public
Mortuary

1

CHATHAM RD

CHOI HUNG RD

The Hong Kong
Polytechnic University

HONG CHONG RD

Choi Hung
Estate

Hung Hom   1000 ft.

1000 ft.

- 1_Jockey Club Innovation Tower
- 4_Chi Lin Nunnery
- 2_Run Run Shaw Creative Media Centre

DISTRICT MAP : SHAM SHUI PO, SHEK KIP MEI, PRINCE EDWARD

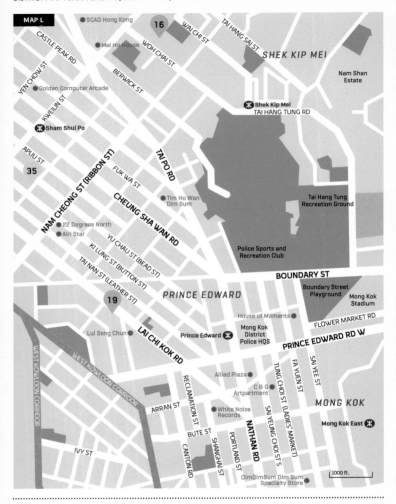

MAP L

- SCAD Hong Kong
- Mei Ho House
- Golden Computer Arcade
- Sham Shui Po
- 22 Degrees North
- Airi Star
- Tim Ho Wan Dim Sum
- Lui Seng Chun
- House of Moments
- Allied Plaza
- White Noise Records
- DimDimSum Dim Sum Specialty Store

CASTLE PEAK RD
YEN CHOW ST
KWEILIN ST
APLIU ST
35
WOH CHAI ST
WAI CHI ST
TAI HANG SAI ST
SHEK KIP MEI
Nam Shan Estate
BERWICK ST
Shek Kip Mei
TAI HANG TUNG RD
16
TAI PO RD
NAM CHEONG ST (RIBBON ST)
FUK WA ST
CHEUNG SHA WAN RD
YU CHAU ST (BEAD ST)
KI LUNG ST (BUTTON ST)
TAI NAN ST (LEATHER ST)
Tai Hang Tung Recreation Ground
Police Sports and Recreation Club
BOUNDARY ST
Boundary Street Playground
Mong Kok Stadium
19
PRINCE EDWARD
LAI CHI KOK RD
Prince Edward
Mong Kok District Police HQS
FLOWER MARKET RD
PRINCE EDWARD RD W
WEST KOWLOON CORRIDOR
ARRAN ST
RECLAMATION ST
BUTE ST
SHANGHAI ST
CANTON RD
PORTLAND ST
NATHAN RD
SAI YEUNG CHOI ST S
TUNG CHOI ST (LADIES' MARKET)
FA YUEN ST
SAI YEE ST
C & G Artpartment
MONG KOK
Mong Kok East
IVY ST

1000 ft.

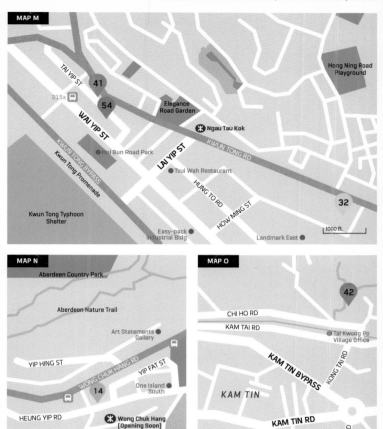

MAP M

TAI YIP ST

41

54

215x

WAI YIP ST

Elegance
Road Garden

* Ngau Tau Kok

KWUN TONG RD

KWUN TONG BYPASS

Kwun Tong Promenade

Hoi Bun Road Park

LAI YIP ST

Tsui Wah Restaurant

HUNG TO RD

HOW MING ST

Kwun Tong Typhoon
Shelter

Hong Ning Road
Playground

32

Easy-pack
Industrial Bldg

Landmark East

1000 ft.

MAP N

Aberdeen Country Park

Aberdeen Nature Trail

Art Statements
Gallery

YIP HING ST

WONG CHUK HANG RD

YIP FAT ST

14

One Island
South

HEUNG YIP RD

* Wong Chuk Hang
[Opening Soon]

Hong Kong
Police College

Pao Yue Kong
Swimming Pool

1000 ft.

MAP O

42

CHI HO RD

KAM TAI RD

Tai Kwong Po
Village Office

KAM TIN BYPASS

KONG TAI RD

KAM TIN

KAM TIN RD

TUNG WUI RD

1000 ft.

- 14_Spring Workshop
- 32_GrowthRing & Supply
- 41_Syut
- 42_O-Veg
- 54_Hidden Agenda

DISTRICT MAPS : **PUI O, LUEN WO HUI (FANLING), SAI KUNG**

MAP P

S LANTAU RD

1,3M,4

● Bui O Public School

CHI MA WAN RD

● South Lantau Community Centre

43

Pui O Beach

Pui O Wan

1000 ft.

MAP Q

24

MA SIK RD

Belair Monte

WO TAI ST

52A, 56A

WO MUN ST

1000 ft.

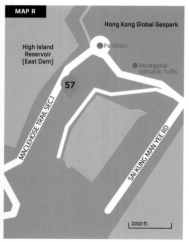

MAP R

Hong Kong Global Geopark

High Island Reservoir [East Dam]

● Pavilion

● Hexagonal Volcanic Tuffs

57

MACLEHOSE TRAIL SEC.1

SAI KUNG MAN YEE RD

1000 ft.

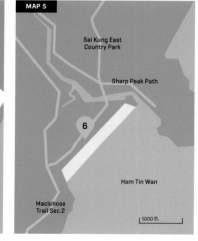

MAP S

Sai Kung East Country Park

Sharp Peak Path

6

Ham Tin Wan

Maclehose Trail Sec.2

1000 ft.

● 6_Tai Long Wan
● 24_Mapopo Community Farm
● 43_Mavericks
● 57_Night Hikes

110

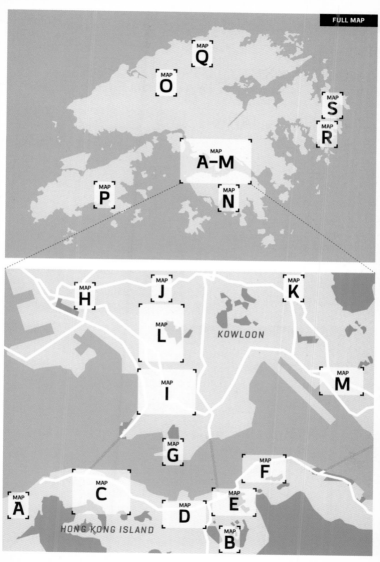

Accommodations

Hip hostels, fully-equipped apartments & swanky hotels

No journey is perfect without a good night's sleep to recharge. Whether you're backpacking or on a business trip, our picks combine top quality and convenience, whatever your budget.

$ < $500 $ $501-1200 $1201+

The Mahjong

An aged *Tong Lau*, where you can get basic services, and occasionally a Moonzen beer in the communal room. In this city, the chance to stay in a chic hostel that doesn't cost and arm and a leg is rare. Pull down the privacy screen and the pod is all yours with your own charging socket and free wifi. Bus stops and great local eateries are on your doorstep.

🏠 1/F, 10-16 Pak Tai St, To Kwa Wan
📞 +852 2705 1869 URL themahjonghk.com $

Mini Hotel

"Mini" means perfectly formed. With prime locations in Central and Causeway Bay, Mini hotel ensures affordable luxury and international delicacies within walkable distance – great after an intense day. Each outpost provides 3–4 types of rooms ranging from 7–11 sqm, with hair dryers, clean linens and LCD TV.

🏠 *38 Ice House St, Central*
📞 *+852 2103 0999* URL *minihotel.hk*

Ovolo Southside

Clean air, greenery and open views are some of the merits you can share here in the affluent Shouson Hill district. But this art-filled converted warehouse has more to offer, such as a 24 hour gym, rooftop bar, free self-service laundry and a shuttle bus service to Airport Express in Central. The new Wong Chuk Hang MTR station is just a five-minute walk away.

🏠 64 Wong Chuk Hang Rd, Wong Chuk Hang
📞 +852 3460 8100 URL ovolohotels.com

Heritage Lodge

🏠 800 Castle Peak Rd, Lai Chi Kok
📞 +852 2100 2872
🔗 www.heritagelodgehk.com

Y-Loft

🏠 238 Chai Wan Rd, Chai Wan
📞 +852 3721 8989
🔗 www.youthsquare.hk/eng/yloft_hostel_rooms

Wontonmeen

🏠 *135 Lai Chi Kok Rd, Sham Shui Po*
📞 *+852 6904 0918*
URL *www.wontonmeen.com*

YHA Mei Ho House Hostel

🏠 *Blk 41, Shek Kip Mei Estate, Sham Shui Po*
📞 *+852 3728 3500*
URL *www.yha.org.hk*

J Plus by Yoo

🏠 *1–5 Irving St, Causeway Bay*
📞 *+852 3196 9000*
URL *www.jplushongkong.com*

Notes

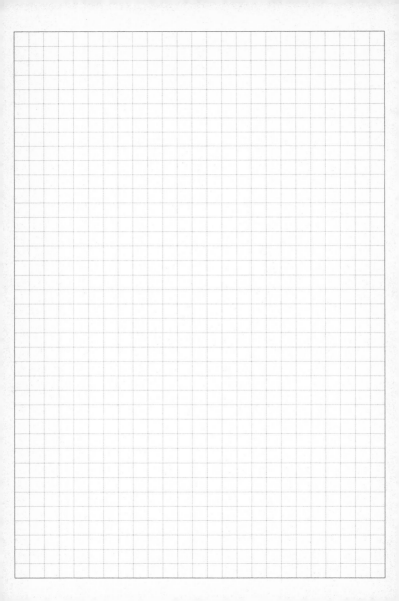

Index

CITIx60

CITIx60: Hong Kong

First published and distributed by
viction workshop ltd

viction:ary™

7C Seabright Plaza, 9–23 Shell Street,
North Point, Hong Kong

Url: www.victionary.com
Email: we@victionary.com
🅕 www.facebook.com/victionworkshop
🐦 www.twitter.com/victionary_
🐾 www.weibo.com/victionary

Edited and produced by viction:ary

Concept & art direction: Victor Cheung
Research & editorial: Queenie Ho, Jovan Lip, Eunyi Choi
Project coordination: Caroline Kong, Katherine Wong
Design & map illustration: Frank Lo

Contributing editor: Elle Kwan, Katee Hui
Cover map illustration: Vivian Ho
Count to 10 illustrations: Guillaume Kashima aka Funny Fun
Photography: The Light Particles

2015 ©viction workshop ltd

Content is compiled based on facts available as of February 2015. Travellers
are advised to check for updates from respective locations before your visit.

First edition
ISBN 978–988–13203–0–8
Printed and bound in China

Acknowledgements

A special thank you to all creatives, photographer(s), editor, producers, com-
panies and organisations for your crucial contributions to our inspiration and
knowledge necessary for the creation of this book. And, to the many whose
names are not credited but have participated in the completion of the book,
we thank you for your input and continuous support all along.